Big Dreams
Big Change
Big Growth

Big Dreams Big Change Big Growth

21 Days to Making It Happen

Celeste Orr

Big Dreams, Big Change, Big Growth: 21
Days to Making It Happen
celesteorr.com

*For big dreamers, trapped dreamers,
and everyone who's almost sure their
biggest, most secret dreams could
never completely come true,*

this one's for you

A Word About Big Dreams & Big Change

Some little girls are never satisfied. They never find outfits they really like, places that feel like their own, or even books they truly adore. It's not that they don't know what they want—they do. They just never find it on shelves, online, or in stores. They're always designing their own outfits in their minds, dreaming about being somewhere else, making up their own stories.

They talk too much in school. They're far too wiggly for a church pew. Their friends think they're too loud, too weird, or too. . . something else, depending on the day.

When these little girls grow up, they hope all this will change. They hope they might fit in better. But they don't. They can't. They're still thinking there's something more.

That was me. It's still me. Maybe it's you too. And maybe you know how frustrating it feels. I was frustrated, too. Until I realized something—my discontent meant I was a big dreamer. That's what yours means, too. And I want you to know something—our discontent can work wonders.

It's not every day that little discontented girls grow up to be women who live out their big dreams, move to foreign countries, buy dream houses and then sell them to travel full-time for fun. They don't often get advanced degrees and then quit good jobs to become artists, writers, poets, or world-traveling experts.

Until they do.
Sometimes they do.

Sometimes those little girls become women who have dreams that won't let them go. They decide it's time to do something about them, and they make a big change.

Maybe you've always been a little odd, felt more than a little left out, and had big dreams swirling in your mind and heart for as long as you can remember. Maybe you've finally decided it's time to do something about those dreams, and you picked up this book hoping it will show you what to do next.

Yes.
A million times yes.

Big dreams become big realities when we make big changes and start to grow in big ways.

Maybe no one has ever told you that kind of thing was available to you.

I'm telling you now.

And we're devoting the next 21 days to making it happen.

Welcome to Big Growth

Brain experts tell us it takes 21 days to hardwire a new habit and make a big change. Just 21 days. That's what we're here to do—to hardwire some new thinking habits that will shift our mindsets and remove the limits we've put on ourselves so we can experience big growth and go after our biggest dreams.

Over the past two decades, I've been chasing a few wild dreams to do impossible things like move across the globe and back again, travel full-time with my family in an Airstream for 7 years, earn advanced degrees, start new careers, create sustainable online businesses, world-school and roadschool my kids, and find a home in my family's favorite spot on the globe. All things I thought impossible until I found myself doing them.

And right now, I'm staring in the face of a few impossible dreams again—

changes I feel called to make but have no idea how I'll ever make happen.

Through it all, I've learned that even when it seems impossible, especially when it seems impossible, the life we've always dreamed of is right around the corner waiting for us to step into it. And the first step happens when we change our thinking by growing new mindsets.

Now I'm on a mission to make that happen for you. Let's do it.

What to Expect

For the next 21 days in this book,
you will have something to read,
something to think about, and
something to process and write about
that will help you move toward
making the big changes you want to
make in your life.

Each day's material will guide you
through an individual mindset you'll
be shifting to help you move past
your ruts and step into your biggest
dreams.

Then, when the 21 days are over, you
will have hardwired a few new ways
of thinking and made some
significant progress toward your big
dream.

I can't promise you'll get it exactly
right the first time through. (Almost
none of us do that unless we've been
sitting on ready for far too long.) But
what I can promise is this — you'll
never be the same.

What If I Get Behind?

Things happen.
Life gets crazy.
We get behind.
I get it.

But there's no behind here. These prompts are yours forever.

They're short and written simply so you can read one each morning before yoga, with your coffee, or over breakfast. But if you miss a day, there's no need to try to catch up or make up for missing. You can pick up where you left off, keep doing one per day, and then finish on your own timeline. You can take breaks. You can even read them out of order if you want. You can go your own way.

Re-read. Re-visit. Re-do. How long it takes doesn't even matter. Don't waste a moment worrying—just do the work and watch your life begin to change. Now, let's get started.

How to Get the Most Out of This Book

The mindset shifts in these pages are meaty. While they're simple to read, you will probably need more than just a few minutes with the concepts to fully benefit from each one.

My suggestion is to read each prompt early in the morning before you start your day as you would read a message from a friend, take a few minutes to think and write about how it applies to your specific change goal, and then watch your mind as it wanders back to the concept throughout the day. Observe your amazing brain bringing the concept to life and putting all kinds of applications to it.

Write down those applications as they come to you. Keep a journal handy and reach for it as often as the ideas come.

You can keep your journey private,
or you can share your thoughts and
parts of your writing with a friend,
an accountability partner, or you can
hop in the email group at
celesteorr.com and share them with
me.

Finally, put some legs on each
concept. As one of my mentors says,
turn your INSIGHT into ACTION
every step of the way and decide how
you will act on each mindset shift,
and then do it. Don't sell yourself
short. Do the work, and you will see
results. Skip the work, and the
results won't come. Get back to it,
and your progress will get right back
on track.

Then, at the end of these 21 days,
join me at celesteorr.com to find
other resources and let me know how
I can support you as you continue to
change and step into your big dream.

Make your change permanent. Take
advantage of every resource at your
fingertips. Reach out. Being here for
you is part of my own big dream.

Getting Ready

Before we get started, you can pave the way for your own big change goal by writing down your answers to these prompts:

Choose your time. What time of the day are you most alert? That might be the best time to make space for these prompts.

Set your intention. What drew you to this book? What change are you hoping to make? Write it down. Put it top of mind each day before you start.

Gather your tools. Do you have a journal or some beautiful paper and pens? Get them ready. Set an alarm. Set reminders. Whatever you need to help yourself make this a priority for the next 21 days.

Set yourself up for the kind of success you can feel good about.

Getting Started

"What if there's more than you know?"

Those were the words that dropped into my heart on a hot summer day back in 2006 – the words that changed everything and set me on a path to realize my biggest dreams in a very real way. Because of those words and my response to them (and if I'm honest, a bit of really good luck), six months later I was living overseas in a place I'd only ever dreamed about and then spent the next 13 years living a travel-rich season with my family that I never dreamed would be possible.

So today, I'm asking you: *"What if there's more than you know?"*

What if I told you that you could find yourself pursuing your own biggest goals and deepest personal desires by shifting just 21 mindsets you didn't know were holding you back?

What if I told you that by tweaking,

adopting, and entertaining just 21 new ways of thinking, you could be ready to go after any change you want to make, no matter how big, or deal with any change that has been thrust upon you?

These mindset shifts have been helping me and my friends and mentors start new businesses, end toxic relationships, start families, travel to dream destinations, and move into new ways of living for years.

More than you know can open up for you, too. Even if it seems impossible. Especially then.

Before we get started with day 1, let's talk about a couple of underlying concepts that are the bedrock to the 21 mindsets we'll cover together over the next 21 days.

Bedrock Concept #1

Our minds are more powerful than we know.

Have you seen the movie *Inception*? It's one of those weird, mind-boggling tales of heartache and drama that will keep you up at night, but it's one of my favorite movies because it highlights how powerful thoughts can be. Even the smallest ones. For better or for worse.

It's true—so much of our reality starts with an idea. A simple little idea.

It could be as simple as "You're so athletic; you should try out for the team" leading us to step into sports at a young age, or something a bit more powerful like "What if we moved across the world for a year or two?" becoming the impetus for a life of international adventure.

Likewise, the "I can't" mindset is just as powerful. If you've ever taken any small child for a walk or hike of any length, I'm sure you know the power of "I can't" firsthand. It's the only way to explain how the same child can hike five miles without a peep one day and can't even manage one mile without whining another. It's the same explanation for why some dreams become reality and others don't.

"I truly believe that thoughts are the greatest vehicle to change, power, and success in the world. Everything starts with thoughts."
—Oprah Winfrey

I've heard this from countless teachers and goal-setters, inspirational speakers and thought leaders. Many call it manifesting your dreams. Some call it having faith in the unseen. Whatever you call it, my guess is you know something about the power it holds. As I write this to you today while living in a reality that was only a far-off dream just a few short years ago, I can tell you I know the power it holds, too.

Take a moment to reflect on your own beliefs.

Do you believe that everything starts in the mind? What events in your life have either helped or hindered you from believing it?

Are you willing to entertain the idea that your life could be different from what you have experienced so far? What are you willing to do to embrace your power for change?

Bedrock Concept #2

We are unstoppable.

I grew up with a lot of angst about missing the boat, mis-stepping, or choosing a partner, career, hometown, life path that wasn't God's will for my life. For years, I tortured myself with indecision, believing that if I didn't do just the right thing at every stage in life, I might mess up my life's perfect plan and live the rest of my days having to make do with second best. So, by the time I reached my thirties and had a husband, two kids, and a scary big home mortgage, I was petrified to go any further. That little belief resulted in a gigantic stalling season in my life where I wasn't moving forward in anything because I was so afraid of making the wrong move. Then I heard a teacher say something that changed everything for me; it went something like this: "It's much easier to get a moving train to change direction than it is to get a stopped train moving again. Go until God stops you. Don't worry if it's not exactly the perfect direction. He'll nudge you onto the right path. Just get going." (paraphrased)

After that, slowly but surely, I got out of my own way and started moving forward, and although I haven't always been exactly on the perfect path every moment of my life since then, I've been moving forward and feeling the nudge in the right direction every day. And no matter what comes my way, I know I don't have to let it make me stuck again. I'm not going to miss the boat because I'm the one driving it, getting new directions as I need them. Only I can decide if it's time to slow down, stop, or keep moving. Otherwise, I am unstoppable.

Here's the thing—You are unstoppable, too.

Nothing can stop you unless you give it permission to. Not debt or fear or guilty feelings or worry or the actions of others. Not your weight or the way you see yourself, not even your current self-criticism. Nothing has the power to stop you unless you let it. Nothing can keep you from the big change you've imagined, so go get it.

Take a moment to reflect on your own beliefs. Do you believe that nothing on this earth can stop you? What events in your life have either helped or hindered you from believing it? Are you willing to step outside of yourself to imagine that you could be an unstoppable force on this earth? Are you willing to see how you might start to believe it and become it?

"Each of us has...
all the time there is.
Those years, weeks, hours,
are the sands in the glass
running swiftly away.
To let them drift through our fingers
is tragic waste.
To use them to the hilt,
making them count for something,
is the beginning of wisdom."

-Eleanor
Roosevelt

I wonder if those bedrock concepts make you squirm a little.

Or maybe you've been waiting for someone to give you permission to think about things in new ways.

Whatever camp you find yourself in today, I hope these next 21 days will make a difference in your life. I hope they'll make it easier for you to change your mind and make a shift. Then make another and another until you're making it all count for yourself as you begin to live a life you love.

I'll be right here cheering you on.

The next 21 days have the potential to change your life.

Are you ready?

I think you are. You wouldn't be reading these words if at least some part of you weren't.

Day 1
I'm going for it

No more: "Who am I to do this?"

I believe in God dreams. Those dreams that pester you until you try them, the ones still hanging around in your soul even after all these years, the ones that just won't let you go. God dreams don't always make sense, but they're always there pulling you to listen to them, to choose a new path toward them no matter how many times you've refused. That's what travel and running my own business from home have always been for me—God-whispers I couldn't ignore. What's yours?

No matter what your dream is, there will always be so many reasons to go after it—and so many reasons not to.

There will always be voices saying, "Who are you to think you could do that?" And sadly, when we listen to those voices and ignore the dream inside of us, it can go quiet for days, months, or even years, and the world misses out on something great from us.

I am a big fan of going after our dreams. It's proven to be something I can't live without. And it starts with deciding to go for it rather than give in to the "Who am I to do this" mentality, even when it's hard, even when that "Who are you" voice has somehow become our own.

Have you always wanted to start a business? Move to a new place? Write? Go back to school? Travel the world? Start inventing solutions to world problems? Stay home with your kids? Climb mountains? Swim oceans? Or do something no one you know has done before?

Make the decision to go for it.

It's true, your business may start extremely small and might eventually have to end to make room for something else. Your books may or may not be published right away.

Your degree may not come like you thought it would. It may take you a while to figure out a way to stay at home with your kids, start rock climbing, get fit enough to swim the way you want to. That part is necessary. But nothing will happen until you decide to start.

Find wisdom. Get training. Surround yourself with friends who will speak life into your dream and help you get there.

But first, you have to decide you're going for it.

Why is this important?

Carrying around a voice in the back of our minds that says, " Who am I to do this?" can sabotage our efforts toward our biggest dreams.

Shifting that voice into "I'm going for it" means we get to experience hope, and hope opens the door to possibility.

Nelson Mandela famously said, *"Everything seems impossible until it's done."* It sounds like he knew a thing or two about God dreams.

I bet Marianne Williamson did, too, when she said, *"Our deepest fear is not that we are inadequate. Our deepest fear is that we are powerful beyond measure. It is our light, not our darkness, that most frightens us. We ask ourselves, 'Who am I to be brilliant, gorgeous, talented, fabulous?' Actually, who are you not to be? You are a child of God. Your playing small does not serve the world. There's nothing enlightened about shrinking so that other people won't feel insecure around you."*

When we capture the "Who am I" thoughts and turn them into "I'm going for it", we're training our brains to see the endless possibilities around us. We're refusing to underperform and shrink into resignation as a person we don't want to be.

It's time to step into every single thing you have the power and capacity to do.

Wouldn't you agree it's about time you went for it?

Write about it

Find some space and time in your day today to write about the things in your life that are stopping you from going after your biggest God dream. Do you think you're too old? too young? not talented enough? not rich enough? What is the thing in your life saying, "Who are you to do something like this?"

Now take some time to write about what it would take to get you to the place where you are ignoring that voice and stepping into that dream. What actions will you take to make it a reality today? tomorrow? next week? next month? What does it feel like to make the decision to go for it? What will this new you do?

Day 2
I trust my
intuition

No more: "No one else is doing it this way, so I must be wrong"

My guess is this isn't the first time you've stepped out and made a big life change. Isn't it weird how no matter how many times we do it, there's still the same old resistance trying to stop us? Whether it comes from well-meaning friends and family members or from our own 3 am worry reels, when you commit to making a big change—albeit around money, location, health, education, whatever—there will be a significant force asking you to stay the same.

There's always that little voice saying you're going way out of bounds this time, getting "too big for your britches", losing your lane.

That just means the status quo is a force to be reckoned with. What it doesn't mean is that we can't or shouldn't reckon with it. It also means you have some people who love you and your changing in any way makes them uncomfortable. They might be worried they're losing the you they know the best. This is normal. It doesn't mean you should stop.

I know the feeling well. When we decided to leave the US and live overseas with our 15-month-old baby in a country where we knew no one, a lot of the people in our life were worried about us. They became worried again when we came home and kept moving around and eventually lived in an Airstream traveling the country for 7 years. And they worried again when we tried to live on a boat and eventually settled down in one of the coldest US states with no harsh winter experience. But that's okay. We had to do what was best for our family— even if no one else was doing it that way.

I bet you know what works, too.
When you're in your groove, I bet you know why. And if you need to change something to go after what's best for your family, I bet you know what you need to do to make it happen. Trust your intuition. Consult experts and listen to wise friends, sure, but don't let them override your gut feelings.

You can trust your intuition.
Go for it. Try it. Make mistakes. Try again. Even if you're the only one doing it that way.

Why is this important?

Carrying around a voice in the back of our minds that says, "Why isn't anyone else doing it this way?" can sabotage our efforts toward our biggest dreams.

Shifting that voice into "I trust my intuition" means we get to experience confidence, and confidence opens the door to possibility.

We must hold tight to this confidence, even when we make mistakes and need to start over again, knowing we can shift and grow and learn. That's part of our knowing, too.

I'm not sure who taught us that we should only do things other people have done before us, or that we should all live our lives the way others have lived before us, but I bet it wasn't someone who made any kind of mark on the world.

If you know your family isn't thriving and you want to try something new to find your groove, do it—even if no one else has ever done it before.

If you know you need to leave your job, start your own business, move to the other side of the world, start a new family tradition, step into worldschooling, or something I can't even imagine for you, do it. Start it. Be the first one.

The world needs what you have to give. So does your family. Even if it's a personal change and you're the only person you know to ever make that choice, do it anyway. Stick with your gut, knowing it'll make you the best you can be for your people—and for yourself.

Wouldn't you agree it's about time you owned your big goals, even if no one else is doing it the same way?

Write about it

Find some space and time to write about the last time you were in your groove with your family. What did it feel like? How did you get there? How did you know you were doing things the right or best way?

Now think about what it might take to be in your family groove every day. How would it feel? Is there an action you can take today to get closer to making that happen? What would it take to grow your confidence so that you could own your big change—even if no one else understands?

Day 3
I don't need to please everyone

No more: "I can't do this—they'll be too disappointed"

I was one of the original people-pleasers back in the 80s. As soon as I was awarded my first academic trophy in the second grade and saw how surprised, proud, and happy my parents were, there was no going back. I lived to make them surprised, proud, and happy.

Most of us like to make people happy, and for the most part, when we're young, single, and independent, we can be pretty good at it. But when we get older, married, have kids, and take on more responsibility, we start making decisions with our own families in mind. And there quickly comes a time to choose between what's best for our own little families and what would make all of our extended family and friends happy.

If you're married and/or have kiddos, I bet you know the struggle well— wanting something so badly but weighing who in your life it will disappoint and wondering if it's worth it. It can be as simple as wanting to spend Christmas Day at home with your kids rather than carting them around to the grandparents' houses. Or, it can be as complicated as needing to move to a new place when all of your family and friends live in the same town— the one that's no good for you anymore. The truth is you simply can't please everyone.

You will either choose what's best for this person or that person, for this group or that group, for yourself and your family or for someone else.

And while there is certainly a lot to be said for selfless choices in some areas of life and love, there is also value in choosing your marriage, your mental health, or your own happiness as a nuclear family, no matter how much discomfort it may cause someone else.

We'll never please everyone, and that's okay. We can do what we know we need to do and trust that the rest will take care of itself in time.

Why is this important?

Carrying around a voice in the back of our minds that says, "If I do that, they'll be too disappointed, so I better not" can sabotage our efforts toward our biggest dreams.

Shifting that voice into "I don't need to please everyone" and even "I choose my kids" or "I choose me" means we get to experience confidence, and confidence opens the door to possibility.

Eleanor Roosevelt said, "Do what you feel in your heart to be right—for you'll be criticized anyway." This quote has brought me peace more times than I can say. Because, let me tell you, I have been criticized more times than I care to count.

And here's the cool thing—the people who you disappoint when you choose your own goals and what's right for your own family are going to be okay. The good ones will eventually come around and might even join you.

Don't be someone who wastes her life trying to please others so much that you never get a chance to become the person you were created to be.

Refuse to do things that don't feel right to you and start doing the ones that do.

I know not every person has the means or circumstances to immediately make a drastic change so that things are better for themselves and their kids. There are all sorts of struggles going on in families with health concerns, finances, people who need to be cared for, and so much more. Just remember that timing is everything, and when the time comes for you to make a decision, knowing it's your decision to make will be critical. Only you can do that.

Wouldn't you agree it's about time you stopped trying to please everyone?

Write about it

Find some space and time to identify an area of your life where you're caught in the people-pleasing trap.

What action can you take today to tear down that people-pleasing part of yourself so that the real you can shine through?

What would you do with the next 5 years of your life if disappointing others wasn't a concern?

Day 4
I know when to reach out for help

No more: "I have to do this alone"

Now it's time to get to the nitty gritty. Think about that one big dream—the reason you bought this book—the change you hope you'll be making when you shift that last mindset and emerge with some new thinking habits.

Would you still go after your big dream if you knew you couldn't do it on your own? If you knew you would reach a roadblock that requires you to ask for help, would you start anyway?

Yes, you totally would because you're here getting a little bit of help along the way. But I often wonder how many big changes and big dreams we've walked away from in the past because we couldn't get to the next

level without someone helping us.
Far too many.

Early on in my non-traditional
lifestyle, I realized the importance of
reaching out for help. Back in 2008,
after living in Australia for a year
and a half away from our family and
friends, it was time to come home.
But as soon as we arrived back in the
States, we realized we were now
completely different people. Our
accents were off, our minds were in a
different place, and we had no idea
how we were going to make enough
money to support ourselves. It was in
those moments that we learned an
important lesson:

Everyone needs help sometimes.
Absolutely everyone. Even if no one
likes to admit it. (Including me.)

How does it make you feel to reach
out for help? Have you found a way
to get the help you need for yourself
and your family and keep your
confidence and dignity intact? Do
you have safe people in your life who
will give you both help and dignity? If

you aren't sure, make a plan before you need it.

You are not alone. You know when to reach out for help.

Why is this important?

Carrying around a voice in the back of our minds that says, "I'm all alone in this" can sabotage our efforts toward our biggest dreams.

Shifting that voice into "I know when to reach out for help" means we get to experience community, and community opens the door to possibility.

The tricky thing about this is it may take more than one or two attempts to get it just right. You may reach out to the wrong person at first, or you may catch the right person at the wrong time.

You may not have a plan in place for the next time you need help, but if you stay open, you will get it when you need it.

You know how to reach out for help. You've done it before, and when you need to do it again, you will. There's no reason to believe you're alone in this change you're making. You've never been alone.

I'm thankful I reached out for help when I needed it. It stirred up my tenacity and determination to help others when they need it, too. And it taught me how to reach out in other areas of life.

Wouldn't you agree it's about time to go after your big dream, even if you know you'll need help at some point?

Write about it

Find some space and time to think about the last time you needed help. Did you get the help you needed? What stopped you? What will you do differently next time?

Now think about that big God dream. Do you need some help to make it a reality? What kind of help do you need (encouragement? coaching? money? time? inspiration? focus? better tools?) What will you do to get it today?

Day 5
It's about more than just me

No more: "I'm so selfish for doing this"

Do you ever feel selfish for doing what it takes to make the big change you want so badly? Has anyone ever told you they thought you were being selfish for doing it? Most of us encounter one or the other—personal resistance or an outright challenge—to the changes we're making. And when that moment comes, we may have to remind ourselves that what we're doing is about so much more than just ourselves.

Something I've found to help with this is setting clear boundaries to get what I know works best for myself and my family (and to avoid what doesn't). But setting those boundaries isn't always easy—and communicating them with grace and honesty is sometimes even harder.

This came up for me when my kids were small and my extended family made it clear that they expected me to do what my parents had done when I was a kid—a weekly Sunday lunch at my grandmother's house 30 minutes away and all holiday meals with both sides of my parents' families. I said no, and it wasn't a popular choice. What I couldn't explain to them was why, so it became a rift in our extended family for a long time.

We don't want to hurt the people we love. We don't want them to misunderstand us. So, sometimes we try to remain small and do what they want so they don't become uncomfortable. But as Marianne Williamson says in the poem we talked about earlier, playing small doesn't serve anyone—not them, not you, not the world. Playing small hurts everyone involved because it keeps the real you—the best you—out of the equation.

You cannot become the person you were meant to be and the person you've always been, too. One of them has to go.

You are not being selfish by making a big change. You know it's about more than just you. Hopefully they'll see it eventually, too, but that's not up to you.

Why is this important?

Carrying around a voice in the back of our minds that says, "I'm so selfish for doing this" can sabotage our efforts toward our biggest dreams.

Shifting that voice into "It's about more than just me" means we get to experience a heart for ownership, and ownership opens the door to possibility.

The biggest place this shows up for many of us is when we realize that becoming more of who we were created to be has a ripple effect that touches everyone we love.

When we step into our full potential and start living with the confidence to own that potential in every way, we change. We're different, and people notice.

Eventually, I was able to seek counseling and identify the reason I had to set boundaries around big family gatherings, even though it was a really unpopular boundary to set and a painful personal discovery. I had to change. I had to step into the me I was meant to be by creating a new family culture and I couldn't do that in the environment I was in.

And even with everyone else telling me I was being selfish for wanting to change in this way, I had to believe it was about more than just me.

All these years later, I can see that I was right, and I'm glad I made the change—misunderstandings and all.

(Even if I wish I had done it with more grace at the time.)

Wouldn't you agree it's about time you embrace the fact that what you're doing isn't just about you and it might just impact a whole lot of other people in a really good way one day?

Write about it

Find some space and time to write about the boundaries you've set.

When and how did you put them in place? Was there any pain involved? How would you do it if you had to do it all over again?

Do you need to tweak anything to achieve better boundaries to make big change easier in the future? Is anything stopping you?

Day 6
It's okay not to
fit in

*No more: "I wish I wasn't so
different"*

I was standing on the beach on Saint
Simons Island in Georgia when I saw
the lighthouse standing tall, proudly
calling to me. I'd been struggling
internally for a few years at that
point, wondering what was wrong
with me and my family and why we
couldn't fit in and be like everyone
else. We were making plans to move
to a town close to Saint Simons, and
that old familiar fear was taunting
me with its same old story. *"You
won't fit in here either, Celeste.
Something is wrong with you. You'll
never fit in."*

But when I saw that lighthouse, these
words came rushing in: *"You, my
darling, were never meant to fit in.
You are something special. You were*

made to stand out, to rise above, to
show the way for others, just like
that lighthouse. And you can't hide it
any more than a lighthouse can."

All these years later, I get chills
thinking about that moment, just like
I get chills when I see women
standing out proudly like that
lighthouse—mamas stepping out to
start their dream businesses or write
their dream books, grandmothers
earning six figures for decades and
transforming their family's finances
or retiring to keep their grandbabies
and take them on weekday
adventures, aunts and friends and
sisters and daughters stepping out
and stepping up to lead, to create, to
revolutionize their lives and the lives
of those around them.

I even get chills when the ladies
stepping up and standing out are just
characters on television like Captain
Marvel when she flies through the
enemy ship, the mom in the Netflix
series *Lost in Space* when she goes
up solo in the weather balloon, and
even *Frozen*'s Elsa and Anna when
they save their entire kingdom.

Here's why—because <u>every</u> woman was created to stand out. All of us. Not one of us was meant to fit in.

Have you ever wished you were someone else, even for one day? I hope after today you won't waste another ounce of your creative, beautiful, wild, weird, and wonderful talent on that again.

You are different from every other human who has ever lived, and that's a really good thing.

You were never meant to fit in.

Why is this important?

Carrying around a voice in the back of our minds that says, "I wish I wasn't so different" can sabotage our efforts toward our biggest dreams.

Shifting that voice into "It's okay not to fit in" means we get to experience our individuality, and individuality opens the door to possibility.

As it turns out, the voice telling me I wouldn't fit in on the coast of Georgia was right—I didn't fit in there any more than I had fit in anywhere else. But you know what? It didn't matter.

When you read that story, did a part of you wonder if those words were only for me and not for you? Did you immediately think, "I wasn't meant to lead the way for others. The change I'm making isn't that big of a deal. I just want to shift and grow a little."

It's okay to feel that way, but if you're reading these words, I can tell you, darling, you were meant to stand out, to rise above, and to show the way for others, too.

And sooner or later, some type of rejection will show up on your doorstep because of it. It's part of being a change-maker.

If you're making a change right now in your life that you can't hide and it's making you feel like the biggest weirdo in your extended family or friend group, relish the feeling. Feel it deeply and let it remind you how much you're changing.

And take some time to appreciate that you've been called to lead the way for others.

Wouldn't you agree it's about time you embrace your weird and wonderful self?

Write about it

One of my favorite women writers Ainsley Arment says, "We are all weird—and weird is wonderful." Make some time and space to write about the ways in which you don't fit in with your friends, extended family, peers, neighbors, whoever.

What do you dislike about not fitting in with them? How could you see this as a good thing instead?

How are you learning and growing through your individuality? What is it getting you ready for?

Day 7
I can reset this as many times as it takes

No more: "It has to be perfect this time"

Have you ever struggled with wanting to get something perfect before you fully commit to seeing it through? If the answer to that question is *no*, you're a rockstar—go ahead and skip to Day 8 if you want. But my guess is you know exactly what I'm talking about. I catch myself doing this all the time. I put off fully committing to a vegetarian diet for 10 years because I knew I'd cheat sometimes. I waited 15 years to start the blog I was meant to start because every first draft was far from perfect. And I procrastinated publishing my first book for 10 of those years because I thought it had to be just right the first time around.

(It wasn't — it had typos. No one minded.) And I wasted precious time.

We can't afford to waste precious time with perfectionism when it comes to making big life changes. We don't have the time to waste. We aren't getting any younger. Our kids are growing up faster and faster every year. And the benefits that will come from making those changes aren't ours until we fully commit. So, as tempting as it is to take tentative baby steps, there comes a time when we have to barrel forward and reset the parts we get wrong.

I learned this the hard way in my twenties by making big announcements to my family about my life decisions and then having to go back to them a few months or years later and backtrack. "I'm going to be a missionary" was replaced with "I'm going to college to be a teacher." "We're moving to Australia indefinitely" became "We're coming home." And most recently, "We're going to live on a boat" became "We're settling down in Maine." And yes, each one of those shifts was a little embarrassing, but guess what? It didn't kill me. And I learned something. I learned that no amount of embarrassment should keep us from making the change we need to make. We get to choose when to reset our path in life. We get to decide when to shift. And we get to do that as many times as it takes.

By now I hope I've learned that nothing is going to be just right the first time around. Nothing. I can always make a shift. I just have to get started. I hope you'll remember that you can, too (especially if the big changes you're making right now turn into more in the days to come).

You can reset this thing as many times as it takes. Each time counts as progress. Just don't stop.

Why is this important?

Carrying around a voice in the back of our minds that says, "It has to be perfect the first time around" can bog us down and sabotage our efforts toward our biggest dreams.

Shifting that voice into "I can reset this as many times as it takes" means we get to experience imperfect progress, and imperfect progress opens the door to possibility.

One of my favorite verses of scripture is, "Abraham didn't tiptoe around God's promise asking cautiously skeptical questions. He plunged into the promise and came up strong, ready for God, sure that God would make good on what he had said." (The Message)

It has big pink marks around it, and every time I run across it, I stop and read it to remind me to plunge headlong into the life I'm called to and trust that God will make it good.

My blog hasn't been perfect since I started—it's always improving. The first book I published had errors in the manuscript when it went to print and over 100 people got copies with errors. My efforts at sticking to a vegetarian diet have been stop and go for years until I finally got into a groove. But you know what? I started those big changes, and I can reset them as many times as I need to.

The change you're making does not have to work perfectly the first time you try it out. You can shift, change, and adjust as much as you need to.

You can reset whatever you need to, as long as you get started. Wouldn't you agree it's about time you embrace your imperfect, wild, and wonderful progress?

Write about it

Make some time and space today to write about a part of the change you're making that you haven't shared with anyone because it isn't perfect.

Write out what you're afraid people will say. Write out what might happen if you never share it.

Then call, text, or email a safe friend today and share it with them, knowing you can reset, readjust, and shift if you need to.

Day 8
I can step back and reassess with my people

No more: "I have to keep going no matter what"

"Can we talk about something?" Who knew five little words could be so powerful? But they can be profoundly powerful, can't they? I've seen these five words save marriages, heal families, and change the world for people. They could even be the words that save you from burning out on that big dream in your heart before you really even get started.

They certainly changed my world just last year.

One day last summer, I was tidying up outside, thinking all was well, when one of my kiddos whispered,

"Mama, can we have a one-on-one? I need to talk about something." So we snuck away to the coffee shop, and he told me what was on his heart. I still tear up thinking about the tears in his eyes and his big-hearted words, "I know you're probably disappointed, but I had to tell you." And I'm still thankful for the response that came, "I'm not disappointed. I'm so glad you told me. I don't know how or when we can make it happen, but I'm going to work on it, okay?"

Truthfully, I had absolutely no idea how because our plans for at least the rest of that year weren't reversible at that point, but I knew we had to try. The only way I made peace with it was to tell him we would go slow and check in again in six months.

Kids have the funniest way of speaking the truth and getting to the heart of things, don't they? As it turns out, two months after this conversation, we were faced with a big challenge and a big decision—we could push through and try to make it work or step back and reassess—

and it was our son who helped us make the decision to step back.

No matter where you are on this path, you can step back and reassess with your people, too. Sometimes we absolutely need to push through, and other times, we need to take some time to reassess. And just like an arrow that's pulled back, we'll go farther than we ever have before.

Why is this important?

Carrying around a voice in the back of our minds that says, "I have to keep going no matter what" can burn us out and sabotage our efforts toward our biggest dreams.

Shifting that voice into "I can step back and reassess with my people" means we get to experience a new perspective, and new perspectives open the door to possibility.

One of my favorite things to do every night is reset my little home for the next day. I tidy up the kitchen, wipe down the counters, plump up the blankets on the couch, and position the pillows and books just right. It makes me feel ready for a new day.

I think we have an opportunity to do the same reset in our souls from time to time, too. Sometimes those resets come from our kids or our partners, and other times, they come from within—like a gentle Spirit beckoning us to tidy up some things and look again.

I'm so glad I listened last year when my kiddo asked me to reassess a few things. It truly has been the arrow-pulling-back moment we needed to launch into bigger and better dreams.

When it comes to your big dream, what areas need reassessing? What have you heard your own people say that might give you clues? (Not the naysayers—just the ones closest to you who know your heart.)

It's a wild ride balancing these big dreams and big changes with our family-loving hearts, isn't it? But there absolutely is a way.

Wouldn't you agree it's about time you embrace your ability to reassess with your family and launch into new territory?

Write about it

Make some time and space today to write about something you reassessed recently—or something you've been needing to reassess for a long time.

How can you tell whether or not it's working? What have you heard yourself and your people say about it over the past 6 months?

What do you feel in your heart to be true about it? If there is conflict, can you find a clear compromise? Write it all down. See what comes to the surface.

Day 9
I keep the big
picture in mind

No more: "Why am I doing this?"

If you've ever started making a big
change and wondered, "Why am I
doing this?" you're not alone.
Everyone who has ever started down
the path of making a big life change
has been tempted to lose the plot and
forget why they started down the
road in the first place. Sometimes
this can be a good thing, causing us to
reassess and reset when we need to.
But sometimes it starts looking a
little too easy to pack it all in and go
back to status quo.

I know because I've done it—so many
times.

A lot of people see my photos on
Instagram and read my books and
articles and think I'm a super lucky
person who gets to live out all of her

biggest dreams. They're wrong. I've walked away from many, many dreams. And although we do often grow out of dreams or let them morph into something that's a far better fit for who we're becoming, I've walked away from far too many dreams simply because I lost sight of the big picture.

Most often what trips me up about making big changes and going after big dreams is money. The money it takes to fund big dreams. The money it takes to keep everything running while you chase big dreams. So when I find a good story about money, I try to hold onto it.

Recently I read a story about how Chip and Joanna Gaines (of Magnolia Homes and Fixer Upper) came very close to going broke and packing it all in before they got the opportunity that changed their lives. They almost missed it. But we know them today because they didn't give up. They kept the big picture in mind, knowing they were meant to turn houses into homes, knowing they were mean to redeem spaces and be a positive voice in the home reno industry. One day it looked like their dream was never going to happen and they just might go bankrupt and have to find a new dream, and the next day it was happening. Just like that. Because they kept going all those years when it was really, really hard.

What trips you up and makes the status quo look better than going after your dreams? What stories have you found that help you keep the big picture in mind?

When we keep the big picture in mind, we are POWERFUL. We don't wonder why we're working so hard or why we started down this path, because the reasons are tattooed on our hearts, written in our journals, stuck to the refrigerator—they're all over the place.

Why is this important?

Carrying around a voice in the back of our minds that says, "Why am I doing this?" can make us lose momentum and sabotage our efforts toward our biggest dreams.

Shifting that voice into "I keep the big picture in mind" means we get to experience a vision of the future, and that vision opens the door to possibility.

Something that always helps me keep the big picture in mind is a phrase my husband likes to throw around (far too much, if you ask me). It's this: "Why not do it right now? We could be dead next year and never have the chance." True. Sobering, but true.

Another thing that always helps me keep the big picture in mind is this quote from The Message: "Clear lots of ground for your tents! Make your

tents large. Spread out! Think big!
Use plenty of rope, drive the tent
pegs deep. . . Don't be afraid—you're
not going to be embarrassed. Don't
hold back—you're not going to come
up short."

I get chills when I read those words
and realize the Maker of the
Universe is telling us to think big. If
you only knew how many times I've
written those verses in my journal,
you might think I was mad. But it
helps me keep the big picture in mind
year after year.

What helps you keep your big picture
in mind and how do you keep it in
front of yourself? Have you written it
in your journal lately? Stuck it to the
fridge in your house? Saved it as a
phone background?

Wouldn't you agree it's about time
you embrace your vision of the
future?

Write about it

Make some time and space today to write about your big picture. Why are you making this important change in your life?

Go deeper, farther into the future than you have before, and write about what life will look like when you've made the change versus what life would've looked like staying at status quo.

Day 10
I label fear, learn, and move on

No more: "That's too scary"

I wake up in the middle of the night thinking I heard something or that I must have forgotten to lock the door, and then when I settle myself again, the questions start scrolling in my mind like I just opened 5,000 emails and 300 screaming toddlers just woke up in my head all at once. It happens every time I take a big step. What about you? Like an old friend, fear hears from the grapevine that we are moving forward and comes to see if she can stop us.

A few years ago, we were offered an opportunity to spend a week on the coast in Oregon—one of our big dreams and a trip that would require us to haul our camper 1,200 miles in just a few days, passing through places unknown to us. We immediately said yes, and then at 3 am the next morning, fear came with her questions: "What if we aren't supposed to do this? What if we get into an accident? What if the weather turns and our pipes freeze over? How are we going to afford all that gas? What if we can't find good places to stay along the way? Will the 101 be too crowded? What if we're too exhausted after six days of driving to enjoy it? What if we don't have enough clothes for the cold wind there?" Then the questions took on a darker tone. "What if one of the kids gets sick? What if I have to fly home unexpectedly and leave my family way out there? What if my husband gets hurt and we have no one to drive the camper? What if I all of a sudden have a bad cold, the flu, cancer, or something worse and we're all the way out there where we don't know anyone?" Perhaps you can relate.

In those moments, we have a choice. We can count this as a sign that what we're doing is too scary and stop. Or, we can label fear, learn from her, and move on. To help me figure out which way is the right one for any particular step, my go-to strategy is to turn these questions into prayers. When I do, pretty soon, new questions start to come, a better "what if" scenario.

Instead, I hear, "What if this is a moment that could change our lives? What if we meet someone there we're meant to connect with? What does the ocean smell like in Oregon? How good will it feel to have the sand between my toes again? Who should we invite to come with us? How much will my kids learn on this trip? What if we absolutely love the rainforest and Pacific Northwest? What's God got up His sleeve this time?" All of a sudden, fear has lost the day and I can move on.

When we exercise our strength, creativity, perspective, and courage in the face of fear, there's no stopping us. We can let fear remind us to be careful and to prepare. We can let her teach us something about ourselves. But we don't allow her to tell us what's too scary. Only we decide that.

Why is this important?

Carrying around a voice in the back of our minds that says, "That's too scary" can sabotage our efforts toward our biggest dreams.

Shifting that voice into "I label fear, learn, and move on" means we get to experience strength, and strength opens the door to possibility.

It can be difficult to know when fear is just being nasty and when there are real concerns we need to pay attention to. The weight on our shoulders and tightness in our chest for both can feel identical. But when we start to see fear as an inevitable part of taking risks, stepping out of the norm, and moving forward on our big goals and dreams, we can label fear, learn from her, and move on without getting stuck.

One of my favorite writers on the topic of putting yourself out there is

Elizabeth Gilbert. I love the way she talks about fear. She says fear is inevitable whenever we take any type of risk, so we might as well give her a spot in the backseat but we absolutely shouldn't let her drive or pick the route.

I love that. Knowing we aren't the only ones facing fear around every corner makes such a difference. We aren't alone.

If your big change is starting to come into view right about now, I bet you've had a visit or two from our old friend fear. The question is, What are you going to do with her when she comes?

Wouldn't you agree it's about time you embrace your strength and tell fear where she can go?

Write about it

Make some time and space today to write about how fear is showing up for you right now. Does she wake you up in the middle of the night or plague you throughout the day? What does she say? What does she bring to mind?

How will you respond the next time fear knocks on your door? Write out your response.

Day 11
I expand my borders and live an expansive life

No more: "There's nothing better out there"

There's an old spiritual song that goes like this: "No limits. No boundaries. I see increase. All around me. Stretch forth. Break forth. Release me. Enlarge my territory." I used to play it on repeat when I was in my early 30s working a job that was growing and stretching me but also frustrating me and trying to make me feel small day after day.

In some way, I knew singing this song was a coping strategy to help me get through my day and treat my coworkers with respect (and not lose my cool, fly off the handle, and sacrifice my family's financial wellbeing). I knew that reminding myself there was more for me and my family just ahead—just in the next season—would help me settle down and get through the present one. But I also knew that this song was more than just a coping strategy. It was calling me to grow, to stretch, to expand my borders and believe things wouldn't always be the way they were.

When you stepped onto this path to big change, I'm sure you were already aware that growth was part of the deal, but have you stopped to think about how that growth happens? Have you started to feel it yet?

Growth happens when we consciously choose to expand our borders and live an expansive life.

Growth happens when we open our minds, our hearts, and our lives and start to believe that the way we've always seen things may not be the only way.

Growth happens when we say yes and move forward, even if we've never gone that way before.

When we embrace growth in this way, we know there's always something better out there for us. And we're right where we need to be to receive it.

Why is this important?

Carrying around a voice in the back of our minds that says, "There's nothing better out there" can stunt our growth and sabotage our efforts toward our biggest dreams.

Shifting that voice into "I expand my borders and live an expansive life" means we get to experience growth, and growth opens the door to possibility.

I love getting together with old friends I haven't seen in years. I can usually tell within the first 30 minutes of our conversation how much they've grown and changed. And so many times, it's like I'm meeting a brand-new person.

With our old boundaries expanded, we can barely even see who we used to be. In our new expansive lives, everything looks different—and so much more is possible.

But here's something not too many people know about this process: It happens in the daily decisions far more often than in those big crossroads moments.

Every time we open our doors to a friend who's different from us. Every time we consider a perspective that's opposite to ours. Every time we say yes to meeting someone new, going somewhere different, doing something in a new way. This is how we expand our borders and live an expansive life.

These words from Eugene Peterson give voice to this compelling call to expand: "I can't tell you how much I long for you to enter this wide-open, spacious life. We didn't fence you in. The smallness you feel comes from within you. Your lives aren't small, but you're living them in a small way. I'm speaking as plainly as I can and with great affection. Open up your lives. Live openly and expansively!"

Wouldn't you agree it's about time you embrace your big, expansive life?

Write about it

Make some time and space today to write a thank-you letter to your past self about how you've grown and expanded your borders over the last 5 years.

How does it feel to see this growth on paper?

Now, imagine you're sitting here 5 years from now. Write a letter to your future self, listing everything you hope you can say you've accomplished on that day.

Day 12
I'll keep working toward my dreams

No more: "I had my chance & it's over"

Not every dream will work out right away. Of course, some do. Some dreams happen suddenly and work out so well we wonder why we didn't try for them before now. But some dreams take a long time to realize. Years, or maybe even decades. Other dreams won't work out at all. (There, I've said it.) It's something you need to know on this path to big, lasting life change.

But here's something you also need to know—It's never over until it's over. As long as we have breath in our lungs and the dream sparking inside of us, it's not over. Some dreams need to die to make room for better ones. Sometimes we'll find a new dream in the ashes of one that didn't work out. Other times, we'll see the same dream emerge out of its own ashes over and over again, calling us forth, drawing us into it. Either way, we get to keep working toward our dreams as long as we're alive. No exceptions.

There's a powerful personal development coach named Brendon Burchard who wrote a book called *The Charge: Activating the 10 Human Drives that Make You Feel Alive.* It's a book that came into my life at just the right time and helped me see the difference between those of us who are driven toward our goals and dreams and those who seem to be sleepwalking through life. The difference is our mindset—a belief that life is meant to be lived, discovered, and meaningful versus a belief that life is stale, redundant, or scary.

You and I are big dreamers, and we know life is meant to be lived, discovered, and meaningful. No matter what happens, we know we

can keep working toward our
dreams.

Recently one of my family's biggest
dreams became crashing
disappointment just a few weeks
after we threw all our eggs into its
basket and stepped toward it in a big
way. The disappointment was
crushing, and the road back was
almost devastating. Except it wasn't
devastating. Once we got through the
initial pain and saw the dust settling,
we felt free. We had gone after a big
dream and discovered it wasn't for
us. (After all, isn't disappointment
just "not the appointment we thought
it was"?) And this became the
disappointment that set us on a
course toward another big dream
we'd been putting off. We hadn't had
our chance and it was over—we'd had
our chance and were free to dream
again.

No matter where you are with your
current dream and your current life
shift, it's not over. It'll never be over.
Even if one dream shifts into
another. You will keep working
toward your dreams.

Why is this important?

Carrying around a voice in the back of our minds that says, "I've had my chance and it's over" can sabotage our efforts toward our biggest dreams.

Shifting that voice into "I'll keep working toward my dreams" means we get to experience hope, and hope opens the door to possibility.

I have quite a bit of experience in this department. There's a big dream in my heart that I've been working toward for over 15 years. I started taking steps in her direction in 2004 and met disappointment and stopped a year later. Then I did the same thing in '07 and '08, and again in '09 and '10. I started to think this was one of those dreams I should just forget about, but it wouldn't leave me alone. It kept rising from its own ashes and calling me forward.

So, in 2014, I took a different approach to this big dream, got myself into loads of personal development circles and took a few tentative baby steps forward, creeping toward my dream a little each day until I finally took a big step last year and another big step this year, and things are finally coming together for me to realize my dream. I'm so glad I didn't believe I'd had my chance and it was over or I would have missed it.

We may not get to decide the timing of our dreams—or even which ones will work out.
But as long as it isn't over to us, we can still keep moving forward.

Wouldn't you agree it's about time you embrace your big, beautiful dreams, no matter the timing of them?

Write about it

Make some time and space today to write about a couple of dreams you walked away from and how you can tell those apart from the one you're working on right now.

Write about how you can feel your mindsets shifting toward your dreams and how making a big change will impact your life for the next 5, 10, or even 20 years.

Day 13
I know when I need to be alone

No more: "I have to be 'on' all the time"

Do you know when you need to be alone? Did you know that knowing that one single thing about yourself can shift all kinds of things in your life?

But gaining this knowledge may require a deep mindset shift for you. You may have been told that the need to be alone isn't real. You may think you need to be "on" all the time for everyone. Or even if you know it's not true, you might be living like you believe it is.

If you're an extrovert by nature, you may need to be alone less than others because you tend to gather strength from others. If you're an introvert by nature, you may need to be alone way more because you recharge best when you're alone. But as long as you're human, you need to be alone sometimes. You need permission to have an "off" switch. We all do.

Some of us go years without realizing we haven't taken enough time alone. For some of us, this is by necessity— we have babies, we're caring for someone with special needs, we're single parenting, we're in the midst of a special circumstance or a busy season, etc. And we find what we need to get through those seasons.

Shifting our mindsets so we can own the fact that we need to be alone sometimes and beginning to know the timing of when we need to be alone is powerful. Guilt-free. It helps us set boundaries and say, "I need to take a walk before I start dinner" or "I need to go out for a coffee. Can you watch the kids for a couple of hours?" or "I'm feeling run down. I think I need to get into bed early tonight. Can you help make sure I do that?" And we rise stronger because of it.

You know when you need to be alone.

You know how it feels to rest, reset, and get rejuvenated to come back a better you.

Why is this important?

Carrying around a voice in the back of our minds that says, "I have to be 'on' all the time for everyone" can burn us out and sabotage our efforts toward our biggest dreams.

Shifting that voice into "I know when I need to be alone" means we get to experience healthy boundaries, and those boundaries open the door to possibility.

Do you know when you need to be alone?

I sure do, but it's not a lesson I learned easily. I spent years pushing through, pounding out the to-do list, getting it all done, and trying to be everything for everyone. It. Was. Exhausting.

So exhausting, in fact, that I burned out. I came back though and quickly learned that I needed to know when I needed to be alone, off the clock, and in recharge mode.

And now, all these years later, I can easily spot the signs. When I haven't taken time to be alone, I get abnormally cranky. I start hiding in the bathroom for a moment of silence. I stop asking for help with things. I get shaky, distracted, and upset at the drop of a hat. I have trouble tuning into my family. But often, one little break alone brings it all back into perspective.

How does your need to be alone show up right now? Can you spot the signs? Your dreams and the change you're making to achieve them are too important for you to burn out just steps before the finish line.

Wouldn't you agree it's about time you embrace those moments when you need to be alone so you can come back and rock the rest of your race?

Write about it

Make some time and space today to write about the last time you took time to be alone because you needed it. How did you know you needed it? What changed for you when you were able to find stillness?

Now make some time and space in your day today to sit alone in stillness—even if it's just for a few minutes. Write about why it's important for you to be alone sometimes.

Day 14
I love a good stretch

No more: "I avoid discomfort"

When was the last time you felt a good, uncomfortable stretch? You know the kind—the ones that make you feel more alive, more awake, more you. They bring discomfort, but it's a type of discomfort you know is making you better and calling you forward.

Do you love it when those stretches come your way? Do you look for them, welcome them, and say a prayer of thanks while they're stretching you? In case that isn't where your heart always lands—in case you'd sometimes rather avoid discomfort (like me), we should probably take care of this mindset shift before we go any further down the path to your big dream.

Here's why—because stretching is the only way to expand and grow. And growing is the only way to bring about big change. When we learn to welcome the stretch, we're welcoming the growth. And the change.

This came together for me when I heard Bishop T.D. Jakes speak in person. It was over a decade ago now, but what he said on that stage still comes to mind every time I'm feeling the desire to run away from uncomfortable stretches and stop my growth. He asked, "What happens when you play the piano and come to the top of an octave? To go higher, you have to start at the bottom of a whole new octave, and then you have to do it over and over again to keep going up. In other words, you can try to stay a big fish in a small pond all your life, or you can grow out of that small pond and become the small fish in a big pond again—over and over and over." (para)

Isn't that the case? To move up in our lives, to go forward, to make big changes, we have to get uncomfortable, swim in uncharted waters, and stretch.

You can learn to love a good uncomfortable stretch. You can feel the burn and love it.

Why is this important?

Carrying around a voice in the back of our minds that says, "I avoid discomfort" can keep us small and sabotage our efforts toward our biggest dreams.

Shifting that voice into "I love a good uncomfortable stretch" means we get to experience expansion and expansion opens the door to possibility.

There's another part of the uncomfortable stretch beyond the stepping-into-bigger-and-better-things conversation, too—it's the stretch of waiting. Sometimes the stretch leads to growth and progress right away, but sometimes, we have to wait for it.

I can't help but think about pregnancy when it comes to the topic of expansion—especially as it relates to being uncomfortable in the waiting.

While pregnant with my first baby around the eighth month, I felt like I was going to be pregnant forever. I also felt like I would keep expanding forever. The end never seemed to be in sight. (Granted, I had gained 50 pounds and he did stay in my womb for 41 weeks and grew to 10+ pounds before birth, so I wasn't exactly unreasonable to feel that way, right?)

But you know what? The discomfort finally ended one August day, and I entered a season of more joy and fulfillment than I had ever known.

That's exactly what the uncomfortable stretch of making a big change can feel like, too—waiting longer than you think you can, stretching more than you think you can, and then—boom. Big change happening.

Wouldn't you agree it's about time you embraced the discomfort, felt the burn, and loved it?

Write about it

Make some time and space today to write a thank-you note to your big, uncomfortable stretch.

If you're feeling one right now, say a big WELCOME and write about why you're glad she's here. Or, if you haven't felt the stretch in a while, let her know she's welcome in your life and tell her why you welcome her and what you'll do when she comes your way again.

Day 15
It really isn't about me

No more: "I really must be selfish"

Wait, didn't we already talk about this? Yes, we did, but this mindset shift is making a reappearance here because it's the one you will have to shift more than once. Maybe even more than twice. My guess is you've been fighting to conquer it this week.

As you grow, change, and expand and start to embrace your strength, as you increase and start owning it, the people around you will notice the change. Some of them may even tell you they don't like it. Your partner might ask what in the world has gotten into you. Your kids may not like that you're taking time for yourself every day. Your friends might start asking if you're okay or if you're abandoning them.

That's okay.

In those moments, it can be tempting to think, "I really must be selfish. Maybe I should just go back to being the me I've always been." Don't do it. Don't go back. Keep going forward. Deep down you know the change you're making is <u>not</u> just for yourself. It's for the people you love, too. Even if they can't see it just yet.

For a gut check, you can ask yourself what you want for your family one year from now, five years from now, or even 10 or 20. Do you want to show up for them as the happiest, healthiest, most alive, vibrant, passionate, and fulfilled version of yourself? Or do you want to show up as stressed out, broken down, pessimistic, and shrinking? My guess is you're shooting for the former, and if that's the case, there's not an ounce of selfishness in the big changes you're making. They will notice the good one day. Keep going.

You are not selfish for your big change. The changes you're making will have a positive effect on your family for years to come.

Why is this important?

Carrying around a voice in the back of our minds that says, "I really must be selfish" can sabotage our efforts toward our biggest dreams.

Shifting that voice into "It really isn't about me" means we get to experience a firm shift and that shift opens the door to possibility.

It's shocking to me how many times personal unforgiveness or false guilt can creep in and sabotage our progress in so many areas of life.

We get into a project, a shift, or a change, and just when we're approaching significant break-through, a voice creeps in telling us we're taking too much time away from our families, we didn't cook a good enough dinner last night, we haven't done anything amazing for our kids lately, and we're suddenly trying to play catch-up for all the things, leaving our momentum in the dust.

The next time that happens, try this: Recognize the voice creeping in and tell it to hold on just a sec because you're too busy doing something that's going to have an amazingly good ripple effect on everyone you love to listen to what it has to say.

Or maybe this: Have your mind so completely set on the fact that the change you're making and the big dreams you're going after are for your family's benefit that the unforgiveness and false guilt voice doesn't even bother trying to get into your head anymore.

I have a note floating around on my desk that says, "Get over yourself or you risk never moving an inch." It's a good reminder that whenever I start thinking the whole world is on my shoulders and everyone I know is waiting on me for something, I'm wrong. Everyone else has their own stuff to handle. I can take time to handle my stuff, too.

Wouldn't you agree it's about time you embraced the ripple effect that's coming and let go of every ounce of false guilt?

Write about it

Make some time and space today to write about the positive effects your big change is already having on the people you love. Or, if you can't see it yet, how do you think it might show up first?

How are you showing up for your people as your true self? What impact could it have this week? this month? this year? this decade?

Day 16
I'll be laughing again in no time

No more: "This is my reality forever"

I have to admit something to you. If you're a big dreamer, you will face disappointment. It will come to you on this path to great things, right between your wins, and here's the kicker—it will be a blessing. Yes, I did just say disappointment will be a blessing. It might actually be the thing that helps you find where you are truly meant to be, and where you'll find the most joy investing your time, talent, energy, and intelligence.

Here's why: Because it's only through the disappointment of some dreams that we're able to find the appointment that's been right for us all along.

I'll give you an example. Up until recently, I'd wanted to be a college professor ever since I met one for the first time. I graduated from college in 2003 knowing I would be back, knowing I would teach in those classrooms one day. Fourteen years (and two babies) later, I returned to pursue advanced degrees and told everyone my intention was to earn my PhD and finally become a professor. It felt GREAT to be in the zone for realizing that dream after waiting for so long. But then, disappointment came. The master's thesis I had spent two years working on was trashed, my graduation was delayed another semester, and I was forced to rethink my goal.

I cried. I hid under a blanket for a little while. I honestly didn't know what to do. Then, something happened that changed my life. In that moment, it suddenly became clear to me that I'd been pursuing the wrong dream all along. It wasn't the PhD and college classroom I desired— it was the teaching. Suddenly I started laughing as I realized I could achieve my teaching dream without a

PhD (which is how you're reading this book right now).

At this point, you may be saying that I should have pushed on despite the disappointment and kept going toward my PhD dream. And truly, that's what I would normally say. That's what I almost did. And it's also completely what we should do sometimes. Sometimes disappointment makes us more determined to go after our dream, more convinced of the life we want. But sometimes, the disappointment of one dream makes another dream come into view so much more clearly. That's what happened with me—I saw for the first time that I was meant to teach without any classroom walls at all. My disappointment had helped me see past my limits.

When you face disappointment, it will not be your reality forever. You will be laughing again in no time, back on the path you were always meant to be on.

Why is this important?

Carrying around a voice in the back of our minds that says, "This is my reality forever" can bring resignation and resentment and sabotage our efforts toward our biggest dreams.

Shifting that voice into "I'll be laughing again in no time" means we get to experience a light heart and a light heart opens the door to possibility.

When disappointment comes to us, we have two choices: We can either feel sorry for ourselves and start believing disappointment is our new reality. OR, we can stand up proudly, look for the lesson, and say, "I'm learning from this. I'll be laughing again in no time" and move on.

In the story I just shared with you about the crash of my PhD dream, some part of me wanted to sink into a "This is my reality forever" cycle. I wanted to think my disappointment meant I wasn't capable, but that wasn't true. I eventually received my master's degree and an opportunity to move into a PhD program. The blessing of the disappointment was when I realized that the PhD wouldn't allow me to study and teach what I know in my heart I was meant to study and teach.

That's just one example from one person's life. My gut tells me there are billions more. What's your disappointment story going to be? Have you let disappointment stall your progress? Or can you already see through disappointment to the appointment awaiting you?

Wouldn't you agree it's about time you embraced a light heart and looked forward to laughing again?

Write about it

Make some time and space today to
write a story about a disappointment
that affected you in a deep way.

Now write about the appointment
that was (or could be) on the other
side. What's possible now that you're
not tied to that other outcome?

Day 17
I don't have to control everything

No more: "It's all up to me"

Have you ever been so completely surprised by something good that it took your breath away? I bet you have.

A sunrise. A sunset. The first time a child says, "I love you". A sweet message from a friend. A clear scan. A check in the mail just when you needed it.

Or what about the time you were at the right place at just the right moment and you were able to experience something wonderful because of it?

The night you met your partner. The job offer that shifted your career. The meal you got to enjoy for free because a stranger paid a blessing forward. The 90-second delay in your trip that saved you from being in an accident. The bird poo that dropped in the spot on your towel you just moved from.

None of those things could have been planned for. And yet, so often when it comes to making big changes in our lives and following our hearts to see our dreams come true, we act like we have to control everything and have a plan for even the smallest of details.

And sometimes that desire for control causes us to miss the good things that have been waiting to surprise us.

This realization came into view for me one winter when I was making family travel plans for a trip out west. As circumstances changed and every one of my plans went awry, I gripped my agenda tighter. Until finally, I collapsed into a heap of frustrated tears and was forced to give in and go with the flow. A few days later I found myself at the top of the Grand Canyon on the very last day before a terrible snowstorm hit that would have prevented us from being able to see her beauty at all, and I knew we were right where we were meant to be—right where we wouldn't have been if I had kept trying to push my own agenda. And I learned to embrace good surprises.

Serendipity is not a dirty word. Beautiful, joyful surprises are on their way to you.

Why is this important?

Carrying around a voice in the back of our minds that says, "It's all up to me" can keep us from good surprises and sabotage our efforts toward our biggest dreams.

Shifting that voice into "I don't have to control everything" means we get to experience surprising joy and surprising joy opens the door to possibility.

I don't think I'll ever be one of those people who leaves everything up to chance. My guess is you won't be either. But embracing a magic we cannot see to experience things we haven't yet imagined is powerful. Especially when we're trying to make changes we can't make all on our own.

I learned this lesson again when following serendipity and little nudges from above led my family to buy a house this year even when we weren't planning on it. It brought us to the showing on the right day to be able to submit a competing offer. It gave me the suggestion from a friend to write a letter to the seller—the letter that won us the bid even though our offer wasn't the highest. It's why we now live in the home we feel we were always meant to live in.

As I write this I can't help but wonder what life would be like if I were in the place I had planned to be right now. According to plan, I should be

working from a boat in the Bahamas
on a wild adventure with my family.
Instead, I'm sitting at a desk listening
to the rain fall outside the window of
a cabin in Maine I now call home,
feeling myself and my family become
profoundly changed by a place we
didn't even know existed a few
months ago. And it feels amazing. So
different from what I had planned. So
much better than I imagined.

It makes me wonder what good
things might be on their way to you,
too.

Wouldn't you agree it's about time
you embraced the joyful surprises
headed your way?

Write about it

Make some time and space today to write about a time when you were surprised by something good.

Now write about something good that might be on its way to you right now—something that will make this change you're making a little easier.

Day 18
I celebrate small wins

No more: "Push. Push. Push."

When was the last time you celebrated your wins—especially the small ones? I mean really celebrated them by doing something out of the ordinary for yourself like taking the day off, booking a massage, going on a hike, eating cake, taking a nap, buying a new book, taking a vacation, . . . (you get the drift)

If it's been a while, chances are you might be having trouble stepping into bigger things, feeling like your growth is at a stand-still. Here's why: When we celebrate our small wins, we learn to appreciate where we were and recognize the growth and forward movement that's happening, and the resulting gratitude propels us forward with new momentum and strength, with eyes wide open to possibility.

I have to admit something to you, though—I'm not good at this yet. As I write these words, I'm struggling with my own big change, feeling stunted in my growth, and battling exhaustion from working too hard at it. I tend to push when I should rest, to brush off compliments and downgrade my progress when I should celebrate, and to focus on all that needs to be done rather than taking time to celebrate how far I've come. And I know it holds me back. My guess is you can relate.

But when we shift our mindset and start recognizing and celebrating our small wins on the way to big change, everything shifts with it. I've seen it happen. It's magic. And I don't know about you, but I don't want anything holding me back.

So today I'm taking time off and finding some cake or a nice, big hunk of dark chocolate to celebrate my small wins. Will you join me?

We're celebrating our small wins, and it's propelling us forward into bigger things.

Why is this important?

Carrying around a voice in the back of our minds that says, "Push. Push. Push." can make us miss a critical step in our growth and change and sabotage our efforts toward our biggest dreams.

Shifting that voice into "I celebrate small wins" means we get to experience gratitude and gratitude opens the door to possibility.

I have a friend whose ability to celebrate small wins is astounding and has completely changed the course of my life. (I'm not even exaggerating.) Her name is Kristen, and we come from such vastly different worlds that I can hardly believe we're friends, much less that she continues to celebrate my small wins with me.

She was a supermodel and now runs an online magazine where she interviews movie stars and thought leaders, and I'm, well, me. But we hop on the phone regularly, and she asks me about how I'm progressing on my goals, and at least once in every conversation, she catches me downplaying a small win of mine and says these words: "Let me stop you right there. Can you roll back what you just said?"

And that one little question stops me in my tracks and helps me recognize that I need to celebrate a small win (or a big one) before I barrel into the next thing.

What about you? Have you caught yourself downplaying your progress lately and wondering what's holding you back?

Wouldn't you agree it's about time you embraced your small wins and get ready to step into bigger ones?

Write about it

Make some time and space today to write about the small wins you've experienced over the past 18 days. Start with the fact that you bought this book, that you've stuck to the material, that your mindsets have shifted.

Now write about the ways you've seen yourself step up, things you've done and thoughts you've had that didn't seem possible this time last year.

Read your small wins and pause a beat before you move onto your next big thing.

Day 19
I'm finding my thing

No more: "I don't know what I want"

Do you know what your thing is? Are you the cooking girl? The book mama? The baby whisperer? The outdoor adventurer? Are you the business mogul? The makeup girl? The health nut? The neat freak?

Do you know what your family's thing is? Are you the sports family? The art lovers? The hikers? The mountain bikers? Are you the family who bakes? The one who homeschools? The one with the rad paintball course in your backyard?

There are loads of ways we step into our things, aren't there? Some of them we choose intentionally, but others seem to choose us somehow. And sometimes we want to change our thing or our family's thing—or both—but amidst all of the things we love to do, the things that define us, and the things we're redefining for ourselves, there's still a part of us wondering if we'll ever <u>really</u> be able to step into our true thing, the one we were put on this planet to do.

In these moments of doubt and wandering (we all have them), we might be tempted to take on an attitude of "I don't know what I want" and either keep going through life on auto-pilot or search for meaning and direction in place after place, career change after career change, hobby after hobby. We may make a big change and then decide we really don't want to go that way and then throw up our hands and say, "I don't know what I want; I'll never figure it out".

In those moments, we have an opportunity to shift our mindset a few degrees and say instead, "I'm finding my thing". It's a subtle shift but a critical one.

"I don't know what I want" can be directionless, hopeless, powerless.

"I'm finding my thing" is motivating, powerful, and full of vision. And the cool thing is we get to choose which way we'll go. We get to decide if we're finding our thing or if we just don't know what we want. We get to choose our own stories. We get to look ahead or remain directionless. I think I know what we'll choose.

We are finding our thing and we won't be searching forever (even if it feels that way sometimes).

Why is this important?

Carrying around a voice in the back of our minds that says, "I don't know what I want" can leave us powerless and sabotage our efforts toward our biggest dreams.

Shifting that voice into "I'm finding my thing" means we get to experience clarity, and clarity opens the door to possibility.

I'm a personal growth junkie. I really can't get enough. That means I read a lot of personal development books, listen to podcasts, and spend time daily journaling, meditating, and on my yoga mat. And do you know the one piece of advice that pops up in every single personal development resource I've spent time with? It's this: We have to know exactly what we want if we're going to get it.

In other words, clarity is queen.

The only way to step into the life we've imagined and have the kind of life we know we were meant to have is to get clear on what exactly that is.

And most of the time, the only way to figure out what exactly we want is to try things that don't work out until we find the one that does.

This is easier in some seasons than it is in others. I can look back on my own life and point to times when I had easy clarity about my life's direction and other times when I didn't. I bet you can, too.

Whether you're in a season right now where clarity comes easy or if clarity hasn't quite reached you yet, you can shift your mindset to know that you're finding your thing. You are not lost and wandering. It's not that you don't know what you want. The truth is, you're finding your thing. You're almost there in fact.

Wouldn't you agree it's about time you embraced the fact that you're finding your thing and get ready to step into it as soon as you find it?

Write about it

Make some time and space today to write about your thing. Own it. If you're already clear on what your thing is, write it out again—you might surprise yourself. If you aren't clear just yet, write until you catch a glimpse of clarity, even if you're only writing questions at first.

Day 20
I'll never give up

No more: "It's time to stop dreaming"

Do you know the difference between the lady who's living a life she loves and the one who spends her days wishing her life could be drastically different? The difference is one is still working, still dreaming, and the other spends her days wishing, comparing, and wasting time.

In Mindset Shift #12, we talked about continuing to work toward our dreams long after we've failed a time or two. Now, as we come to the last couple of mindset shifts, it's time to talk about what kind of tenacity it will take for you to not only keep working toward your dreams, but to keep dreaming, too. It's going to take both.

It's in you. (Yes you)

But you may start wondering how to know when too much is too much. When the whole world is telling you to give up, be satisfied, and "bloom where you're planted", you may start wondering if it's time to get real and stop dreaming.

When that happens, I like to look at history for some guidance. You've heard how Thomas Edison failed over and over again on his way to creating the light bulb. (Sources number his failures somewhere between 1,000 and 10,000.) But did you know that not only did he not give up until he achieved his light bulb dreams, but he also continued dreaming and working after the light bulb was a success and went on to patent over 1,000 successful inventions that revolutionized the way we communicate, use electricity, and even watch movies today? Did you also know he was kicked out of traditional school and had to be taught at home by his mother because of "mental deficiencies"? My guess is he didn't waste a moment wishing his life could be different; he was too busy working and dreaming to even think about that.

You won't give up. You're way past wishing now.

Nothing can stop you.

Why is this important?

Carrying around a voice in the back of our minds that says, "It's time to stop dreaming" can sabotage our efforts toward our biggest dreams.

Shifting that voice into "I'll never give up" means we get to experience tenacity, and tenacity opens the door to possibility.

In case you need more than one example from history of someone who can give life to your determination to never stop dreaming, I want to offer this:

"Never give in. Never give in. Never, never, never, never--in nothing, great or small, large or petty--never give in, except to convictions of honor and good sense. Never yield to force. Never yield to the apparently overwhelming might of the enemy." — Winston Churchill

You will know when those convictions reflect your own good sense and lead you to shift gears and go a different way, to focus more on one dream than another for a season, or to change course and embrace a new dream altogether. But the determination to never give in— never, never, never, never—that is something to last a lifetime of big dreams, big changes, and big growth.

Wouldn't you agree it's about time you embraced your never-give-up spirit and kept on working and dreaming?

Write about it

Make some time and space today to write a story about future you—how you almost gave up on your dream, but you decided to try just one more hour, just one more day, just one more year, and that was when you saw the breakthrough you'd been working toward.

Look back at the work you did for Mindset Shift #12. Are you ready to not only keep working toward your dreams but to keep dreaming, too? Write about the difference between the two for you.

Day 21
I love my small beginnings

No more: "I'm embarrassed this is all I can do"

I can hear your questions, dear one. I've had the same ones myself so many times. "What if my best is too small? What if I put it all out there and it's just not enough?" These are the questions that come every time we're right on the edge of breaking through to our biggest dreams. Trust me—I've asked them a thousand times.

Every time I start stepping toward a new dream, it feels like a fire in my bones for the first few days. It's a rush. The excitement of it is intoxicating. It sweeps me up and washes away everything on my mind. I gain a new perspective on life, and my heart feels like it's soaring. I talk faster, I can hardly sleep, and my mind races with all kinds of new ideas. I try to write them all down, but my hands won't move fast enough. I can't concentrate on anything else. I believe I can do anything, and it feels like something amazing could happen at any moment.

Then, I start inching forward and take my first few baby steps. I put myself out there the first few times, start comparing my first steps with everyone else's and the overwhelm hits. I hear a voice telling me I can't do it. "*It will never work. Who am I to think it could? I don't have enough time or help or skill or talent. I'm too old. I'm not good enough. I have no idea how to do this. Can I back out? What was I thinking?*" This is the point where shifting one little mindset to recognize small beginnings and start loving them is critical. When I don't, I never move forward. When I do, nothing can stop me.

You won't let your small beginnings hold you back. You've started down the path toward something you know you were meant to do. There's no turning back now. Next year's version of you is looking back through time saying, "Don't give up. Keep going. It will all be worth it." It's time to step toward her.

Keep dreaming, dear one, keep working and dreaming. Fall in love with your beginning—no matter how small it feels.

Why is this important?

Carrying around a voice in the back of our minds that says, "I'm so embarrassed this is all I can do right now" can cause us to stop trying and sabotage our efforts toward our biggest dreams.

Shifting that voice into "I love my small beginnings" means we get to experience confident humility, and confident humility opens the door to possibility.

The term "small beginnings" is one I found in Scripture: "Does anyone dare despise this day of small beginnings? They'll change their tune when they see [him/her/them] setting the last stone in place!" (The Message)

Loving our small beginnings is something that can give us immense peace when we start moving toward our goal and start getting to know others on the same path. It's the only way I know how to quiet the voices that say, "*Your efforts aren't as good as hers. Your attempt is child's play. You'll never be as good as she is. Everyone is laughing at you for trying to do this.*"

Those voices come to everyone. The truth is everyone is not laughing at us for trying to do anything because they're too busy thinking about their own stuff.

What's also true is it's not fair to judge our first attempts based on someone else's fifth or fifteenth or fiftieth, and everyone knows it. (If they don't, you can tell them.)

Embrace those small beginnings of yours. It's the only way forward. "Clear lots of ground for your tents! Make your tents large. Spread out! Think big! Use plenty of rope, drive the tent pegs deep. . . Don't be afraid—you're not going to be embarrassed.   Don't hold back— you're not going to come up short. . ."

Wouldn't you agree it's about time you embraced your small beginnings so you can blow past them?

Write about it

Make some time and space today to
write about your small beginnings.

How are you celebrating where you
are?

Go back to the top and make sure
you're getting it all down. Be sure
you're making a record of where
you're starting so you can look back
in one year, five years, or twenty
years and see how far you've come.
You'll only be able to do that if you
start to love your small beginnings
now. Do it. You won't regret it.

What Happens Now

You may have woken up this morning with the sinking feeling that you've finished these 21 days of mindset shifts and you're still not entirely where you want to be. Your big dreams, big change, and big growth may not be fully finished just yet. The good news is there's a reason for that. The bad news is that very reason — we never fully arrive. No one does.

There will always be another part of your big dream, big change, and big growth to reach for. Some would say that's what keeps us alive. I would say, at the very least, it's what keeps big dreamers like you and me living our fullest lives. If that intimidates you more than just a little bit, here's another piece of good news — we never have to go alone. There's always help.

Here are a few of my favorite books for big dreamers. They can help you. Let them help you.

- <u>Big Magic</u> by Elizabeth Gilbert
- <u>The Artist's Way</u> by Julia Cameron
- <u>Everything is Figureoutable</u> by Marie Forleo
- <u>You are a Badass</u> by Jen Sincero

And if one of your big dreams is to put a book or a piece of artwork or some other big project out into the world and/or you're into building better habits to make things happen for you, these are the books that helped me get over the finish line to publish the book you're reading right now:

- <u>The War of Art</u> by Steven Pressfield
- <u>Atomic Habits</u> by James Clear

When You're Ready to Go Deeper

Maybe you've reached the end of these 21 days and you know in your heart you need to retrace your steps to get each mindset shifted firmly. Or maybe you want to revisit certain days and work on the two or three mindsets that are proving particularly sticky for you. Follow your heart, dear one.

Then, when you're ready to go deeper, there's one little trick you can use to propel you forward. The trick is this —writing about it.

You can use these next few pages to explore other mindsets that may still need shifting, and to get clear on what big dreams, big change, and big growth means for you.

Go Deeper #1 — Write about it

What does your ideal day look like? (the one where you're living your dream life already)

You wake up in the morning and . . .

Go Deeper #2 — Write about it

What part of your ideal day can you do today? What part of your dream life are you already living?

Go Deeper #3 —
Write about it

If you already have some part of the
life you want, what exactly don't you
have? Get specific.

Now, why don't you have this
already? What's holding you back?

Go Deeper #4 —
Write about it

Challenge your beliefs. Ask yourself, "What if nothing is actually holding me back from living my dream life other than myself?" Now write the steps you could take to get there.

What items on the list have you attached an "I can't" to? Use the space below to make a list of the people you know who have overcome those obstacles.

Go Deeper #5 — Write about it

What parts of your dream life <u>don't</u> you want? What parts confuse you? What are the down sides to the life you're hoping for? What are you subconsciously afraid will happen if you get all you've ever wanted from life?

Why are you going ahead anyway? What is pulling you forward?

Last, But Not Least

Surely every writer must be a lover of good books and good teaching, determined to let the ripples of influence received from another flow out from herself. That's me, and those good writers and teachers are the teachers, writers, and authors whose stories have shaped mine. Thank you.

There are others, too. Friends and colleagues who have crossed my path, impacted my life, and influenced me in ways that have found their way into this book. Thank you. Thank you for sharing your life in a way that makes every dream a very real possibility.

And of course, there are my people. Dee, the way you keep growing and changing is worth writing 1,000 books about. Thank you for being you. Matthew, I still forget about everything every time I get around you and that's what makes everything possible for me. I can't imagine being me without you. Thank you for being mine. Elijah & Malachi, you're what it's all about for me, my sun, my moon, the brightest stars. Thank you for coming into my life and letting me stay in yours. Mom & Dad, I'll always be thankful I was yours. Thank you for everything. Harmony, Ella, Easton, and Cohen, you're going places, big places, and I'm glad I get to be your Aunt Bop Bop. Thank you for sending so much happiness my way. Email group friends, you deserve so much honor. Without you, I wouldn't be writing. Thank you for every Friday morning you've shown up with me. & God, I know now more than ever before that you love big dreams and have so much more for us than we could ever imagine. Thank you for being so much bigger than we can know right now.

And last but 100%, certainly, entirely not least . . .

You, dear reader. Thank you for investing in this book. Thank you for investing in yourself by really showing up here. Thank you for putting your heart into these pages. Thank you for overlooking my mistakes and soaking up the good bits. Don't be mistaken— If you have the resources to read this book, chances are you already have what it takes to change your mindsets and start living the life you've always imagined <u>and</u> love your people well while you do it.

It's true, not all of us will get there. But since you've read this far and are still reading, I have a feeling about you in particular, though. You're going to get there. You may need to switch things up a few times along the way, but you'll see. It will happen. Then, when you need to, you'll start all over and get there again.

Thank you for inviting me to be a part of your big change.

One more thing
This isn't the end.
Not even close.

Stay on the path.
Keep going.
Start over as often as you need to.
Rest when you need it, but never
stop.

If they can do it, so can we.
If you've read this far, you're already
doing it.
Never stop, dear one.
Never.

As you keep going after your dreams,
I'd love to hear your story and stay
connected to you through my Friday
morning email group.
You can join for free at
celesteorr.com/subscribe.

I hope to see you there this Friday!